Affiliate Marketing

Earn A Living As A Productive Amazon Associates Or Click Bank Marketing Affiliate

(Leveraging The Power Of Social Media To Boost Your Profits)

Moises Stephenson

TABLE OF CONTENT

Introduction 1

Innovative New Procedures And Equipment 2

Some Suggestions To Help You Get Begun 6

Do Not Engage In Affiliate Marketing. 15

Marketing Affiliates On Amazon 23

Ai Marketing Tools Have Become Crucial To Business Expansion. 26

Why Affiliate Marketing 39

Understanding The Crucial Elements Of List Construction 49

Three Qualities Your Personalized Affiliate Marketing Websites Should Possess 54

Training On Affiliate Marketing 67

Standard Jargon With Which You Should Be Conversant. 96

Setting Up A Link Shortening Service 101

Why Affiliate Marketing Is The Most Effective Way For Beginners To Generate Income. 104

Utilize Free Report To Boost Affiliate Sales .. 113

The Affiliate War: Strategies For Victory 119

Your Affiliate Website 128

Getting Set Up 134

Introduction

Due to how simple it was in the past and how difficult it can be now, many believe that blogging is a vanishing art. That is the furthest thing from the truth. Despite the need for a few additional skills in the modern blogging era, blogs are still highly regarded for their ability to provide readers with fascinating, educational, entertaining, and meaningful content. In addition, many bloggers who began within the last year or two earn tens to hundreds of thousands of dollars from their blogs. There is still opportunity for achievement in this industry.

Whether you are starting a blog because you have a passion for writing or because you want to earn money from it, we will cover it in the following chapters. If you are prepared to get started, why don't we jump right in?

Innovative New Procedures And Equipment

Combining the immense sales that can be generated by cultivating a large following with the VOLUME generated by moving numerous physical items makes selling various products (digital, services, and physical) a significantly more effective strategy. In addition, if you have a diverse selection of affiliate offers on your website, you can include "pie in the sky" sales if you so choose. Could you possibly provide me with an example of this? One time I even made a transaction by promoting an MBA program with an affiliate link! This was made possible through the use of the EDx affiliate program, a prime example of the type of program you will need to enroll in if you want to earn money. What is the difficulty? Juggling and managing so many moving elements! In order to gain access to the most lucrative affiliate networks available online, significant businesses utilize tools that simplify this process and grant them access. Methods of utmost significance for the development of affiliate marketing Genius Link is one of these devices. Using Genius (https://www.geni.us), you can join affiliate programs for multiple accounts at once. With this method, adding funds to the various Amazon locales is a breeze, and it functions flawlessly with Amazon. Worry not about losing customers due to regional differences; each link will transport readers to the Amazon site for their region. Many additional applications, including Barnes & Noble, Best Buy, and iTunes, are available for installation. You can create an Amazon affiliate link directly from this page by copying the URL of the product's sales page and pasting it into the text field provided. If you are using Chrome and have installed the appropriate plugin, you can access this feature by selecting the button on the website itself.

Another option is Trakonomics (available at https://www.trackonomics.net). This instrument serves a similar purpose, but significantly expands the number of available affiliates. This page lists products comparable to EDx. In addition, Trackonomics enables you to search across multiple affiliate accounts for products and then employ the option that generates the most revenue. So, if you're in the business of selling smartphones, you can now evaluate the potential earnings difference between selling the device through Amazon or directly from the manufacturer. This is superior to Best Buy and all other options on the market! In both programs, clicks and transactions can be tracked, allowing you to determine which of your connections are the most popular, whether a link is unavailable, and how much money you've made during a specific time period. The only drawback? The exorbitant monthly fee for Trackonomics is $500. There is, however, a free demo version available.

However, using Genius Link is entirely free.

Many additional solutions are available for those who desire a more straightforward business plan and sales funnel, but these will help you increase your affiliate earnings. Using Google Analytics to monitor the efficacy of your website and its individual pages is one example. You can monitor your site's performance in search engine results for different keywords, make adjustments to better its organic search engine rankings, and then observe the site's traffic, conversion rate, and affiliate commission earnings. The same holds true for landing pages; A/B testing software can help you optimize your page so that conversions skyrocket.

Some Suggestions To Help You Get Begun

1. Establish your affiliate marketing objectives

Before launching an affiliate marketing campaign, it is essential to have a firm grasp of your objectives. What do you hope to accomplish? Do you wish to increase your number of prospects or sales? Or perhaps you wish to increase brand recognition or expand your customer base.

Regardless of your objectives, it is essential to define them before beginning. This will help you create a more targeted and effective campaign, allowing you to ultimately achieve your desired results.

Not certain where to begin? Consider the following concerns when defining your affiliate marketing objectives:

- What are my overarching business objectives?

- What am I hoping to accomplish with my affiliate marketing campaign?

- Who is my intended demographic?

What type of message do I wish to convey?

- What action do I desire my intended audience to take?

You'll be well on your way to establishing a successful affiliate marketing campaign if you take the time to answer these questions.

2. Conduct research

Before beginning affiliate marketing, it's essential to conduct research. There are numerous affiliate programs available, and they are not all created equal. Some programs have more favorable terms and conditions than others, and some may not be accessible in your country.

Before you sign up for an affiliate program, you should thoroughly review the terms and conditions. Pay close attention to the commission structure, payment schedule, and other specifications. Ensure you fully comprehend everything before agreeing to it.

Affiliate marketing can be a great way to make money online, but only if you do your homework and select the correct program.

3. Determine the optimal affiliate program

There are affiliate programs for virtually every conceivable form of product or service. How do you determine which affiliate program is the best fit for you and your business, given the abundance of available options?

Consider the following factors when selecting an affiliate program:

What kinds of goods and services does the affiliate program promote?

Has the affiliate program earned a positive reputation?

How simple is it to use the marketing materials for the affiliate program?

What type of commission is offered by the affiliate program?

Is the customer service of the affiliate program responsive and helpful?

By taking the time to consider the aforementioned factors, you can select an affiliate program that is a good match for you and your business.

16. Be tolerant

Affiliate marketing is a great method to earn money online, but getting started requires time and effort. Be patient and do not anticipate success overnight. Affiliate marketing online can be an excellent method to earn a full-time income, but getting started requires time, effort, and commitment. Be patient and do not quit if you do not see immediate results.

17. Persevere

Don't abandon your affiliate marketing objectives. You will ultimately achieve success if you persevere. Affiliate marketing can be a lucrative way to earn money online, but getting started requires time and effort. Do not become disheartened if you do not see immediate results. A successful affiliate marketing enterprise, like Rome, is not built overnight. You will ultimately see the results of your labor if you persist.

18. Test, test, test

Test, test, test. This is essential for affiliate marketing, as you must determine what is effective and what is not. Determine what yields the best results by trying various methods. Testing is the only way to determine what works and what does not.

19. Never cease studying

Continue conducting research to enhance your marketing skills.

Be prepared to exert yourself

Never cease investigating new Opportunities.

21. Be malleable

As an affiliate marketer, you must be adaptable in order to keep up with the ever-changing Internet landscape. This entails being receptive to new opportunities and adaptable when necessary. You will be able to remain ahead of the competition and maximize your affiliate marketing efforts if you are adaptable.

Do Not Engage In Affiliate Marketing.

I believe it is essential for you to know this at the outset so you can avoid making some of the errors that I and many others have made when getting started.

First, you should avoid constantly chatting with your friends and family on social media to generate sales. You may discover some good, long-term customers because this group already knows, likes, and trusts you, and if you are helping to solve their problem, then that's fantastic!

The issue here is the persistent sales pitch. It's a quick way to lose friends and alienate family if you only speak about selling something when you interact with others. However, if your offer would be ideal for a cousin, it may not harm to mention this.

You should also avoid sending new friend requests to individuals you knew in the past with the intention of immediately selling to them. I cannot count the number of times complete strangers have added me on Facebook and then immediately pitched me their course or product. It is the worst experience, and I delete them immediately.

If you use this type of aggressive sales technique, your account may be flagged, and you will be unable to use social media for legitimate business if it is removed.

To this point, if you anger your friends and family on social media by pushing a product they don't want on them, these people will be wary of conversing with you and won't want to hear what you have to say when you have your own product to sell. Because you only sell, they won't be willing to give your product a try or assist your business.

Approach your family and acquaintances with caution.

The next thing you should avoid doing in your affiliate marketing business is sending people directly from your content to the affiliate website. By doing so, you will become an anonymous third party and will not be able to develop a relationship with your audience.

In this book, you will learn how to acquire email addresses from individuals prior to sending them to your affiliate offer, thereby creating the opportunity to establish a long-term relationship with them.

Lastly, you should avoid appearing like an oily-haired car salesman (no offense to car salesmen, but your industry has a terrible reputation). This leaves individuals with a bad taste in their mouths. Once you have all of your systems and automations in place, if you use your power and time to manipulate people into purchasing from you solely for financial gain, you will damage your relationships with your audience, tarnish your reputation, and make less money in the long run.

Money is not the purpose of what we do; it is a byproduct. This topic is elaborated upon in the following section.

Your One Job

Therefore, we are not permitted to spam our links across the internet, implore family and friends, or trick people into purchasing something that is overpriced or unnecessary.

Then how do we generate income?

You should now view your position as an affiliate marketer, or as a seller of anything for that matter, as being the person who solves people's problems by offering the best solution.

That is all.

That is your sole duty.

The fundamental objective of this position is to provide people with solutions to their problems, despite the presence of numerous strategies and tactics.

In affiliate marketing, we accomplish this by identifying products in which we have faith, which will assist people, and then locating individuals whose problems we can solve.

The benefit of affiliate marketing is that we do not need to first create our own product, so we can immediately begin assisting others.

In later sections, we will discuss how to plan our strategy for assisting people and the various vehicles you can use to reach those in need of assistance.

When we invest our heart and soul into assisting a specific group of people in achieving their objectives, it becomes simple for them to pay us money.

Because of this, money is the byproduct. Helping comes first, then money follows naturally.

Imagine that your child is beginning to demonstrate natural piano talent. If you do not know how to play piano, how much would you be willing to pay for a course taught by an expert who specializes in teaching piano to children? You are not required to learn piano beforehand, nor are you required to tell your child no. This course becomes quite beneficial.

How much would you be willing to pay for training from a business professional who has already relocated to Italy, mastered the language, and flourished in their new position? Your employer should be responsible for paying for that course.

Lastly, you're probably reading this book because you're aware that people are making money online, but you don't know how to get started, and you don't have a lot of time to start the process and presumably quit your miserable 9-to-5 job.

This is the reason I'm composing this book. To resolve your issue. I've been in your shoes and have spent over five years learning how to make money online. I would like to abbreviate that period of time for you and others because 5 years is far too long to continue doing something you detest.

By assisting you and reducing the amount of time required to complete this task, you can learn to assist others, and that seems like a very worthwhile objective to me. As previously stated, money is always a result of assisting.

For the time being, know that your sole responsibility is to assist others in resolving problems.

Marketing Affiliates On Amazon

Amazon is the world's leading e-commerce platform.

Amazon features hundreds of millions of products and has more than 300 million active consumers.

Amazon's affiliate marketing program allows you to refer customers who purchase products from Amazon to your website.

You can become an affiliate marketer if your blog posts, videos, social media posts, or other forms of content have helped people find what they're searching for on Amazon or purchase something they found useful.

The affiliate marketing industry has existed for a number of years, but Amazon's 1998 introduction of its affiliate program altered the game. Affiliate marketers can now earn up to 15% commission on every sale they generate.

Internet marketing is another name for affiliate marketing. It is a contract between an affiliate and a merchant that stipulates the affiliate will receive a commission for any transactions or leads resulting from their promotional efforts. Amazon's affiliate program is one of the largest in the industry. Amazon compensates its affiliates via visits or impressions.

There are two levels of the Amazon affiliate program: associate and professional. To qualify for the associate level, a merchant must generate less than $10,000 per month in sales from their website outside of Amazon, have a website with at least 100 unique visitors per day for 14 consecutive days, and agree to post at least four times about Amazon products on their own social media platforms. A professional has high production requirements, such as 1 million unique monthly visitors and 10,000 Facebook followers, but can leverage Amazon to acquire more.

Amazon does not provide affiliate marketing as a service, but the Amazon Associates program allows consumers to make money by referring customers to the Amazon store.

Users can earn money in a variety of ways, including by adding connections to other websites, linking to products on their website, and receiving commissions on sales generated by referrals from outside sources.

Ai Marketing Tools Have Become Crucial To Business Expansion.

The goal of utilizing AI tools for business development is bolstered by AI's ability to accelerate decision-making and production. In a similar fashion, it boosts the revenue of businesses. It also promotes brand development and audience targeting. Above all, it expedites the transformation of information and data with minimal errors.

The advantages of utilizing AI have previously been discussed. A great deal has been said about AI and its contribution to enterprises' revenue growth. Every business has objectives and a strategy for achieving them. The application of AI in business enables people to forecast sales, and marketers can predict sales based on consumer behavior by systematically analyzing customer data. When AI is deployed with the appropriate strategy and vigor, these feats become feasible.

Observe a few of the artificial intelligence (AI) tools that can aid in the success of affiliate marketing campaigns.

Jarvis

We are aware that content is a vital component of affiliate marketing campaigns, and Jarvis is one of the most popular AI copywriting tools that assist in the creation of impressive copies for these campaigns. GPT-3 is the natural language processing technique that the software uses to generate highly persuasive versions. It includes copywriting templates that facilitate the creation of appealing and effective copies. In addition, it facilitates the production of SEO-friendly headlines, meta titles, and meta descriptions.

The application enables users to concentrate on the marketing aspect of the task while handling the copywriting space with simplicity. This instrument makes it simple for users to discover excellent content ideas.

The free trial period provided by the tool provides novices with an excellent opportunity to test the tool and become acquainted with some of its outstanding features.

GetResponse

GetResponse is one of the most effective affiliate marketing platforms. Additionally, it has vast applications in email marketing and digital marketing campaigns. The highlight of the GetResponse tool is its feature-rich GetResponse Conversion Funnel, which facilitates the creation of remarkable landing pages and email marketing campaigns. It provides consumer support around the clock and accelerates web design. Users are offered an extended 30-day free trial without requiring a credit card.

Pictory

A well-designed affiliate campaign can aid in the expansion of your business. If you want to astound your audience, use Pictory, an AI-powered video creation tool. My friend, you need to reconsider your video production if it consists solely of a decent background and a few arresting poses.

A great video requires a script, captivating music, the proper footage, and excellent editing. Pictory can provide all features to its consumers. Creating videos of professional quality is as simple as clicking a button, and your affiliate marketing campaigns can yield multiplicative results.

This tool makes it simple to convert text to video. Using the tool's remarkable features, visuals to videos can be converted. Additionally, the users are pleased with the results, as editing makes the videos more appealing and professional. The feature of automatic caption generation saves users time. The ability to trim videos and add audio enables users to create captivating content for marketing purposes. And if you're still looking for more, try out the numerous templates in the dashboard that are just waiting to enhance your tool experience.

Frase.io

Frase.io is another compelling and remarkable product in the field of AI affiliate marketing tools. Frase is unrivaled in its ability to facilitate the development of an affiliate marketing website, which is a prerequisite for success in this industry. SEO has become, in recent years, the dividing line between effective and ineffectual marketing campaigns. Unless the campaign generates interest on the Internet, the intended results cannot be achieved.

Understanding The algorithm employed by Google enables users to maintain a competitive advantage over their peers. Frase's AI-driven algorithm comprehends the optimal use of keywords to generate compelling and engaging affiliate content. It is straightforward to improve your rankings and obtain the desired results from your affiliate marketing campaigns.

Utilizing the instrument to develop an effective content strategy is beneficial for consumers. Analyzing the campaign's overarching strategy provides insight into its success. Monitoring your accomplishments also allows you to stay ahead of the competition. It offers a seven-day free trial to beginners with no credit card required.

ManyChat The primary objective of affiliate marketing campaigns is conversions. But your responsibilities do not end there. You should make an effort to engage your customers. Chatbots are the most efficient means of interacting with and satisfying consumers. ManyChat is, as its name suggests, one of the most effective AI-powered chatbots for optimizing marketer consumer engagement. Chatbots are the most effective method to engage website visitors. With the assistance of chatbots, consumer inquiries are resolved effectively and results are obtained. In addition, the chatbot's automated capabilities make it a highly effective tool for websites. Additionally, it increases traffic generation. The intelligent features of ManyChat include appointment scheduling, email monitoring, and intelligent remarketing.

ManyChat is simple to configure and integrate with social networking sites. Social media platforms are among the most frequently visited by users. ManyChat is for you if you want to provide your consumers with a personalized conversational experience. It has emerged as one of the most cost-effective solutions for affiliate marketers as a result of its exceptional functionality. It is a totally free platform.

Optmyzr

Optmyzr is among the best affiliate marketing platforms because it provides an all-in-one solution for PPC campaigns. The platform evolved over time and granted users multiple advantages. Paid advertisements are one of the most prevalent and popular affiliate marketing formats. It is possible to optimize marketing campaigns if the tool is used to generate effective results.

Lead generation is one of the many advanced advantages that can be obtained by utilizing Optmyzr. The most intriguing aspect of the instrument is that it has existed for over 20 years and is still in use.

Voluum

Tracking the performance of the affiliate marketing campaign is a crucial step. If the campaign is not measured and monitored, it is difficult to determine whether it was successful or unsuccessful. It also aids in maintaining affiliate data and measuring its performance. Achieving optimal management of affiliate marketing campaigns can be facilitated by making informed decisions.

The utility enables users to accurately and efficiently monitor the campaign's results. If you are a novice, you may find it challenging to use Voluum. However, if you are an experienced affiliate marketer, this is the solution for you.

Any one of the aforementioned AI tools offers the optimal combination of innovative features, ease of use, and data management.

Article Publicity

When most people consider search engine rankings, search engine optimization (SEO) comes to mind. The haste to manipulate algorithms in order to achieve higher search engine rankings. SEO is overrated and has become excessively challenging.

What is the actuality?
People who are searching for anything, such as hair loss products, weight lifting information, or home business opportunities, enter specific search phrases into the browser. The WORDS that people use to search have a substantial effect on your results.

The Key Effectiveness Index ranks the search terms used to find product X. They obtain sites X through N because the terms they searched for are prevalent on those sites (either in the meta elements at the top of the page - which you cannot see - or in your content) (typically the top 25 words, as this is what the search engines crawl). What relevance does this have to article marketing?

You'll be surprised by how straightforward this is, as anyone can perform it competently. Free distribution of your articles on marketing, home business prospects, training, etc. to other websites, blogs, and eZines constitutes article marketing. FREE? Yes, for nothing! Because, in exchange, you will receive a concise bio and links to your website in the "resource box" at the end of the article. Your content will adhere to a subject that you select. Therefore, if you want to write about affiliate marketing or blogging, you should link to a site that is most closely associated with your topic. As an affiliate, if you do not have your own website, you will likely have access to one through the business you have chosen to promote.

What an excellent opportunity to write about becoming a marketing expert or about lead generation! This identifies YOU as the expert and provides you with a multitude of benefits, such as lead generation, increased website traffic, and improved search engine rankings.

Due to the popularity of this type of marketing, you can find software programs and websites that enable you to easily syndicate your content to hundreds or thousands of other websites.

Consider how many people you could introduce to your organization!

As an illustration, consider the following: Jane Doe, a marketer, posts an article on the web-based article distribution service iSnare. Jane chooses to pay $2 even though submitting to them is free. Her message was forwarded to over 150 additional distribution lists, which then forwarded it to numerous other lists. Within a few weeks, Jane's article (which she

Googled) yielded approximately 650 results. 650 additional websites shared and linked to her site's content. THIS IS A SIGNIFICANT NUMBER OF LINKS. There are numerous opportunities for team formation.

Your content should be well-written, focused, easy to understand, and beneficial to your audience. If you openly promote your product or service, nobody will use it. Provide a link to your website in the resource field. Other links in your content should be avoided, as editors will remove them. Subtlety is the key to composing these types of pieces. Internet business expansion is greatly aided by discretion.

Here are some resources that will assist you in getting begun with article marketing: Examples include iSnare, The Phantom Writers, and ArticleMarketer. If you Google "article distribution services," you will find hundreds of websites where you can publish your article. You may choose to spend money on this, but if you do, you should conduct thorough research to identify the most cost-effective solution. Depending on the circumstances, you may even be able to do this for gratis. This is an excellent strategy for achieving your goals!

Regardless of the style you select, it should be unique to YOU and written in your own voice, enabling your personality to shine through. One of the pillars of relationship marketing is getting to know your prospects and letting them get to know YOU.

Why Affiliate Marketing

Since I already had experience developing a website for affiliate marketing, I opted for that.

This time, I thoroughly investigated the affiliate marketing industry. I used a step-by-step guide the last time I did it. I had no idea that so many companies offer a percentage of the profits for each transaction.

I researched blogs, YouTubers, and even took a good-looking Udemy course. But it was incomplete; not all processes were shown.

Some of them were too focused on selling you products to educate you how to get started. Others have missed crucial aspects. In addition, to make matters worse, there were internal contradictions.

I realized that no one could tell me what to do and what actually works because they lack the necessary knowledge. Affiliate Marketing, like all other industries, operates through trial and error. There isn't a recipe.

I began my affiliate marketing business with a notepad by my side. Documenting everything I did, what worked, what didn't, how I overcame obstacles along the road, etc.

The notebook is used to create this volume. I structured it, made it more adaptable to various methods of operation, and streamlined it.

How-To Manual

These posts are extremely beneficial and simple to compose.

- If you sell white adhesive, you might want to explain how to use it to create a craft.
- If you sell fitness equipment, you could write about how to use it and exercises that incorporate it.

- If you are selling oven cleanser, you could write about how to use the product to clean an oven.

Utilization of the item yields a profit

These posts are more difficult to create because they require purchasing the product, using it, and writing a review post.

You can also create videos.

However, these kinds of posts are highly valued by customers. Attempt to construct one occasionally.

You will still have to compete for a position in search engines if you do it initially. And there are still many important tasks to complete on your website.

Final advices

- Don't let perfectionism immobilize you. You must write a quality post, but it need not be flawless. Remember that you can return at any time to make the necessary adjustments.

- Read and evaluate the comments, but do not feel threatened by them. The greatest source of information about your business is the competition. Therefore, read extensively and gain a great deal of knowledge, and then, if you deem it appropriate, implement what you've learned to your business.

- You are adequate; do not undermine yourself by believing otherwise.

- Be mindful of self-sabotage.

- Do not fear failure, and do not attempt to predict the future, as humans are incapable of doing so. Start, do your best, and let the world inform you whether your product is sufficient or needs improvement.

What qualifications are required to become an affiliate marketer?

Anyone can participate in affiliate marketing. There are no standard requirements.

However, knowing how to write a blog post, string together a fantastic review, or do video is a huge advantage because it means you don't have to pay for content at first. Additionally, any marketing knowledge you already possess will be of great benefit to you.

HOW TO FIND THE BEST AFFILIATE PLATFORM, PART FIVE

You presumably began your blog with the intention of making money in the future.

And when it comes to monetizing your blog, affiliate marketing is one of the most effective methods for converting traffic into income.

However, affiliate marketing is only a viable strategy if you can discover high-quality products that your site's visitors are interested in and that you are proud to endorse.

1. ShareASale

ShareAsale is among the most prominent affiliate networks available.

ShareASale houses affiliate programs for over 4,500 merchants, both large and small, whereas Amazon Associates is solely concentrated on Amazon products.

ShareASale's dashboard allows you to sign up for all of these merchants, generate connections, and view your statistics from a single location.

Note that you must individually apply to merchants and receive approval from each merchant, which is fairly typical for an affiliate network like this one.

ShareASale is an excellent platform for selling both digital and physical products.

On the digital side, for instance, there are numerous WordPress theme and plugin businesses, hosting providers, etc.

And on the physical side, there are numerous large and minor merchants. There are also thousands of other small and large enterprises, such as Warby Parker (sunglasses), Sun Basket, Wayfair, Reebok, and NFL Shop.

Essentially, regardless of the niche of your website or blog, you can likely discover offers worth promoting.

What you must know about ShareASale Niche/product categories: There are both physical and digital products available.

The average commission rate depends on the merchant with whom you sign up.

The duration of a cookie depends on the merchant you register with.

Minimum payout: $50

Awin (previously Affiliate Window)

Awin, a shortened version of Affiliate Window, is another prominent affiliate network that provides access to over 13,000 merchants.

ShareASale was acquired by Awin in 2017, but the two companies continue to operate as separate entities with various merchants.

With over 13,000 merchants, Awin offers a wide variety of physical and digital products.

Among the notable celebrities are:

Etsy

AliExpress HP XE (transmission of funds)

StubHub

Under Armour

Gymshark

You will also discover a large number of smaller merchants in a variety of niches.

Awin was founded in Germany, so the merchant list has a slight European bias, though there are also many American and international companies.

Similar to ShareASale and CJ, you will be required to register individually to merchants within the network. You can then generate links and begin monitoring statistics.

Affiliate Marketing's Past

The misconception that Amazon invented affiliate marketing is widespread. Affiliate marketing was founded in 1989 by the world's first web advertiser and marketer, William J. Tobin. Additionally, William J. Tobin founded PC Flowers and Gifts. He conceived the entire concept of affiliate marketing and advertised his program on the Prodigy Network. He devised an affiliate marketing scheme that entails paying a percentage of each agreement or sale to the Prodigy Network. By 1993, Tobin's affiliate marketing strategy was generating Prodigy more than $6 million annually. This achievement prompted Tobin to present his idea to the world in 1996. However, it was not officially recognized until the year 2000.

In 1994, CDNOW created the BuyWeb Program, which was based on the concept of music websites evaluating new albums by musicians and then linking to CDNOW so that visitors could purchase the albums if they enjoyed them.

Amazon's associates program was launched in 1996, well after CDNOW's debut. Despite Amazon's reputation as the pioneer of affiliate marketing, it launched its program well after CDNOW's launch. Despite being the first to establish the concept, they were the first to attract global attention to affiliate marketing as a whole. The proposed model was identical to the others in that the marketer was compensated based on a percentage of the selling price of the goods. This paradigm has since become the standard for all affiliate marketers.

Understanding The Crucial Elements Of List Construction

Leads from Affiliate Marketing

Once you begin using affiliate marketing, generating leads will be one of the primary concerns you must address. Email addresses are a common source of leads because they represent actual individuals who could become your members, subscribers, or customers. Possessing a robust list of prospects ensures the ability to reach a profitable market and profit from it.

Importance of affiliate marketing lead generation

Businesses that sell products or services spend billions of dollars on advertising alone. Yes, there are millions and billions. Spending such a large amount of money is primarily motivated by a desire to promote a product, expand its market, and ultimately increase sales.

In affiliate marketing, the affiliate company is responsible for the relatively modest advertising expenses. As an affiliate, this is therefore not your concern. Your only obligation is to find a market to promote to that will receive you favorably and pay you in exchange.

This market will consist of affiliate marketing prospects, as opposed to a traditional business. Your success in affiliate marketing will hinge on the quality of these leads and the quantity of positive feedback they generate. When someone says, "The money's on the list," or something similar, they are referring to the list of prospects. Without it, you have little chance of selling, much less generating money.

Increasing your affiliate marketing prospects

Affiliate marketing is not particularly complicated, but it can be challenging nonetheless. It's a tried-and-true business strategy, and many affiliates have found success with their chosen programs. Similar to other businesses, your success in generating affiliate marketing leads will depend on a number of factors. Consider the following factors carefully:

Your reputation

As a beginner in affiliate marketing, you will discover that it will take some time before you can generate affiliate leads. This is something that every new marketer encounters, as gaining a substantial following takes time.

In order to attract a significant number of affiliate marketing leads, you must establish your brand as a reputable entity in the industry. If you lack a reputation, potential prospects won't be able to trust you or do business with you. If you had to choose between a well-known marketer and an unknown one, wouldn't you rather purchase from someone you know as opposed to a complete stranger?

Your affiliate marketing prospects are similar in nature. Before they will agree to purchase, enroll, or become one of your recruiters, they must view you as a trustworthy merchant or affiliate.

Web traffic

The number of visitors to your website has a significant impact on the number of affiliate marketing leads you can generate. High website traffic is advantageous in two ways: it enables you to obtain affiliate accounts that are proportionately larger and increases your likelihood of generating additional affiliate marketing leads. You may first need to focus on implementing website-building strategies, or you may need to join a networking service that offers affiliate programs.

The affiliate item

Two factors determine the success of your affiliate marketing lead development. One is the item's value, and the other is your comprehension of the product.

Every affiliate must meticulously select their affiliate products. A proven or at least probable affiliate product with robust sales will be much easier to market and generate revenue from. Since consumers are more likely to respond to it, affiliates will find it easier to generate leads using it.

Gaining more leads requires a thorough comprehension of the affiliate product's desirability and value. If you can explain why and how a product works on your website or in your articles, you will be able to sell it more effectively, particularly in comparison to competing products vying for the same market.

The market segment or target

Affiliates are typically concerned about market saturation, which occurs when a particular market area is saturated with identical (or at least comparable) products and services. It becomes increasingly difficult to market, let alone convince potential customers to consider the product or service you're endeavoring to promote.

You can avoid this, however, by focusing on generating affiliate marketing leads from precisely targeted market groups or niches. Consider marketing or selling products to a specific demographic that shares a common but largely unmet need. Because there is little competition in this industry, you will find that, with the right strategies, it can be quite lucrative.

Three Qualities Your Personalized Affiliate Marketing Websites Should Possess

It is not sufficient to know what type of affiliate marketing website to create. Whether your website sells a single product or a variety of products, each one must satisfy specific criteria for success. Your unique affiliate marketing website should include:

Friendly to users. Create affiliate marketing websites that are intuitive for users. Maintain links and buttons' visibility and use frequency.

2. PERFECTLY FORMATTED Utilize a layout or structure that functions well with the product you're attempting to sell. Never make the mistake of designing an affiliate marketing website for large motorcycles (such as Harley Davidsons) with a design that incorporates delicate insects and flowers; only a fool would attempt this.

3. ORGANIZED. Place the appropriate links where they are most likely to be seen without interfering with other elements to maintain the organization of your affiliate marketing websites. In addition to categorizing your links, you should also categorize your products (don't just place all of your links in one category). Maintaining order on your website will encourage visitors to continue exploring and eventually depart.

The Google Penalty Checker by Fruition

According to Fruition's Google Penalty Checker, affiliates are frequently the most affected by Google algorithm modifications. Fruition won't be able to prevent it from occurring, but it will be the most effective instrument I've ever used to explain what occurred. When coping with a decline, it is essential to understand why your rating fell. This free application will illustrate this to you.

Paid affiliate marketing tools

Flippa

Use Flippa if you want to bypass the steps required to create an effective affiliate website from scratch. This website is a bidding-based marketplace for the purchase and sale of domains (think eBay for websites). Flippa allows affiliate marketers to acquire domains with a robust backlink profile in order to expedite SEO development.

ShareASale

The first stage in ShareASale affiliate marketing is forming partnerships with websites in need of sales. We have examined several affiliate networks, including C.J. Affiliate and Impact. ShareASale is our primary affiliate partnership resource.

ShareASale connects publishers and advertisers who need assistance generating sales. Publishers may receive payment for each call, inquiry, or website visitor they generate for an advertiser.

Affiliate marketers would earn significantly larger commissions per transaction if they worked directly with advertisers, but ShareASale is an excellent starting point.

SEMRush is our tool of choice for keyword research, SEO error resolution, and competitor analysis. I've been using this program on a frequent basis since 2012, so be warned that I'm biased!

This tool is essential for marketers who wish to assess on-page SEO issues and identify the content that generates the highest ROI for competitors.

Grammarly

Grammarly is essential for individuals who frequently publish content on their affiliate websites. Grammarly is an enhanced variation of your standard spell checker.

Grammarly does not just flag spelling errors. In addition, it highlights grammatical errors, such as misspelled words and improper comma usage.

This program's accessible version is utilized by our group. However, the commercial version has significantly more in-depth content review capabilities.

Marketing strategies for affiliate

Select the appropriate partners.

Even now, word-of-mouth marketing is an effective strategy. Obviously, you would want to investigate prospective affiliates with loyal and engaged audiences. In addition to numbers, you should consider engagement, rapport, authority, and page visits when making decisions.

In addition, you must determine whether the audience is intrigued in the products you are selling. Determine your area of expertise and partner with affiliates whose interests align with yours or whose audience falls within your target demographic. If you're a tech company, you wouldn't want to employ someone who specializes in pet supplies.

Enhance your systems.

Although your affiliate network may drive traffic to your website, conversion should be your number one priority. In other words, site visitors should be sufficiently engaged to take action, such as making a purchase or subscribing to a newsletter.

Expand your affiliate program's reach.

To mitigate risk, investors diversify their portfolios. The same principle applies to growing your affiliate program. Although relying on one or two affiliates is an excellent starting point, it may not be sustainable in the long term. Creating a diverse affiliate program is the most effective way to maximize the true potential of your program. With its aid, you can reach out to foreign audiences and cultivate new prospects.

Utilize discount coupons

Even if they save only a few dollars, consumers desire a bargain. Because of this, coupons continue to gain popularity in digital marketing. According to statistics, sixty percent of all internet consumers actively seek out coupons prior to making purchases from virtual stores. People are using the Internet more frequently due to the coronavirus outbreak, making saving money a top priority.

Establish brand-to-brand partnerships

In 2017, 34% of marketers ranked co-branding as the top strategy for increasing email subscriber numbers. According to a PartnerPath survey, 68% of consumers use co-marketed advertising to make purchases, even if they have to speak with a salesperson.

Affiliate marketing erroneous beliefs

A functional affiliate marketing program necessitates the configuration of a number of distinct components, but the process is generally straightforward. If you have the knowledge and technical skills necessary to run your business, you can surely figure out how to create and manage an affiliate program.

Concerning your affiliate marketing software, you should not be concerned.

Referral tracking may appear complex and sophisticated, but its implementation is straightforward. If your website is fueled by WordPress and integrates with AffiliateWP, you can quickly and easily set up your affiliate marketing program.

Some individuals may believe that managing an affiliate marketing program is extremely challenging, but the opposite may also be true.

As we have seen, establishing an affiliate program is simple. It does, however, require an ongoing commitment of resources. Affiliate marketing is not passive in the conventional sense, nor is it always straightforward. You get out of life what you put in.

Affiliate marketing depends on strong relationships between program administrators and affiliates, which necessitates some maintenance work. It takes time and dedication to get to know your partners and what works for them, to provide them with useful resources, to adapt your procedures to market changes, and to maintain a marketing strategy for your affiliate program.

Traffic is not equivalent to money in affiliate marketing (or any other form of digital marketing). Even if your affiliates convey thousands of interested visitors to your website, it will be for naught if you fail to convert them.

In affiliate marketing, your marketing efforts and those of your affiliates are combined. While others may contribute, you are ultimately responsible for converting visitors into buyers.

To accomplish mutually beneficial affiliate partnerships, your landing pages must have a reasonable conversion rate.

The more you employ cutting-edge technologies such as Affiliate Landing Pages, the easier this will be.

Training On Affiliate Marketing

There are numerous seminars on how to become an effective member. A portion of these are free, but the majority of the finest require payment. If you are serious about finding success with affiliate marketing, you should be willing to invest in instructional classes that will assist you.

You must purchase a partner marketing instructional class from someone with a solid history and reputation in the industry. John Crestani is an authentic example of a person with a distinguished past and reputation. He consistently earns a substantial amount of money as a partner.

John Crestani's Super Subsidiary Framework course is exceptionally well-known. This is a 6-week program where you will learn everything you need to know to have a successful partnership.

The Super Associate Framework will provide the following benefits:

I. Piecemeal subsidiaries promote success

Choosing the optimal specialty

The finest Affiliate associations

Identifying the finest proposals for advancement

Avoiding Member Advertising Errors V. Sites and Deals Channels VI.

Powerful techniques for generating targeted visitor traffic (web crawlers, YouTube, solitary promotions, online entertainment, and more).

Promotional campaigns that believer

IX. Million-Dollar Swipe Record in which John reveals his earlier successful partner campaigns

X. Attained for your channel pages.

A coordinated conversation with John Crestani

Admission to the enigmatic neighborhood that will assist and support you

Additionally, significantly more...

There is no aspect of successful member showcasing efforts in which

John Crestani has close to no knowledge. The Super Member Framework has numerous testimonials from satisfied customers and is the most effective subsidiary advertising preparation available.

In the following section, we will examine the most frequently used member marketing language...

Exceptional Markets

The most effective subsidiary advertisers target unambiguous niche markets. They create a website centered on their chosen specialty and provide an incentive to their customers through happiness. Commissions can be obtained by elevating member offers pertinent to the specialty.

It is crucial to choose the proper specialty. You want to ensure that there is sufficient interest in the specialty and that it is profitable. These are the most popular specialties where money is assuredly made:

1. prosperity creation
2. Health and wellness (for example, weight loss)

3. Personal development

These specialties are typically well-liked. There are numerous member offers in these three specialties. However, these three specialties are also extremely serious, so it is prudent to seek out other lucrative specialties. Utilize a combination of keyword research and methods to demonstrate that money is changing hands in the specialty (are there partner offers available?).

Pay-per-click advertising

Google and Bing, among others, are frequently regarded as the finest sources of website visitors. This is because clients enter a specific search term (catchphrase) to discover what they need. As a subsidiary, you can purchase pay-per-click (PPC) traffic from Google or Microsoft to direct specific visitors to your offers.

Historically, pay-per-click (PPC) traffic was very inexpensive, but it has become significantly more expensive over time. Traffic from Microsoft properties, such as Bing and MSN, is typically less expensive than Google PPC. You should do the math in this situation. Paid traffic is an excellent method for testing adjustments to offers, as you can typically start receiving targeted visitors within minutes.

Profit from Speculation (return on invested capital)

If you are spending a lot of money on ancillary advertising, you should be aware of the venture's profitability. Deduct all mission expenses from the net income (bonuses) that you accept. This will quickly reveal whether your missions are productive and to what extent. You need to achieve the highest possible rate of return on your investment.

How to Turn Your Affiliate Marketing Business into a Profitable One familiar with various programs. Take the example of Digitstem for this discussion.

In addition to providing a very attractive commission rate of 50%, the program also provides a cookie that is valid for 60 days, increasing the likelihood that you will earn further money. The majority of users do not make decisions about their education on a whim. Nonetheless, you do not need to be
concerned about losing your commission while they are considering the options they have since there is plenty of time and there is no need to rush!

Digitstem now provides more than 900
different courses on a wide range of subjects, and the number of offerings is always increasing, so you can be certain that there is something for everyone.

Investigating affiliate programs should also include putting their goods and services to the test to determine whether or not they are worth promoting. Even if a certain vendor has a high commission rate, an Copyright © 2022 || 17

How to Turn Your Affiliate Marketing Business into a Profitable One outstanding support system, and a strong reputation, there is still a possibility that you will not find the product helpful or interesting. This is the case even if the vendor has a solid reputation. Something like this may occur very frequently: even if a product seems to have excellent qualities and a strong social presence, it may not be appropriate for you and the people who follow your content, and that's perfectly OK. But if you don't test them and find the problem in time, all your work will be for nothing: the audience won't follow your advice, and it's hard to win back their trust once you've lost it. If you want to do some research on your rivals, you can join a variety of affiliate marketing forums and platforms, or you can just read the blogs that are written by affiliate marketers.

Pick Your Affiliate Marketing Methods

Informal exchange is as yet a viable showcasing instrument. Normally, you'd need to investigate potential affiliate who as of now have a drawn in following that confides in them. As such, decide your specialty and work with affiliate under a similar field of interest or who have a group of people that matches your objective fragment. Assuming you're a tech organization, you would have zero desire to pick a affiliate that has some expertise in pet items.

Create a website for your affiliate business. Direct traffic to your site, your main goal should be conversion. That is, when visitors land on your page, they should be engaged enough to take action, whether that's to purchase a product or sign up to your newsletter. Conversion optimization creates a great user experience, which increases leads and traffic to your website. Other optimization strategies to boost conversion include:

Creating video information, Sending personalized email messages, Using intent-based keywords on all your website pages, Developing targeted landing pages, Producing highly relevant content or updating previous ones and Testing your platform speed

affiliate marketing products

OK, that is sufficient speculative talk... how would you really get begun and turned into an affiliate marketer?

Indeed, first you will require an item. To get this, you are going need to go to a site like JVZoo or Commission Intersection. Another great one is Clickbank.

Here, you'll have the option to see a huge determination of various items that have affiliate programs. Simply look at and search for the ones you're keen on. You'll find that you can see some data with respect to the various items, so attempt to search for things that are selling at a fair cost and proposition a decent commission.

A few destinations will allow you to see a harsh number of deals, in which case you obviously need to search for the things that are selling great.

Whenever you've recognized the item you might want to advance, you then need to contact the proprietor. On the off chance that you are fruitful, they'll furnish you with your connection and you'll be allowed to involve that as you pick.

Another thing to remember here however, is that many affiliate items will incorporate showcasing materials alongside them. Keep in mind: assuming you are getting along nicely, that implies that the maker is getting along admirably. They have a long list of motivations to need to see you succeed what's more, in that capacity, they will give things like messages, a deals page, flag promotions and different materials by and large.
Assuming that you're somebody who is totally new to the universe of showcasing, then I enthusiastically suggest that you pick an item that offers these sorts of rewards. Along these lines,

you can make ready in a flash by just reordering the materials you've got.

You ought to then see yourself sell in similar numbers: it's the same item and a similar showcasing routine... so there's no reason that it shouldn't work comparably well.

Like I said previously: this is in a real sense a 'reorder' business model. Another person as of now has the item selling great with a set framework, all you are doing is duplicating a similar framework yet ensuring it's your ledger that will get the pay.

Building a Store:

Assuming you are selling various affiliate products (which is likewise very good strategy), then, at that point, you can construct a store to sell them from. That implies that you'll feature and advancing items that are applicable to your image as you would do in an web based business store. The main genuine distinction is that when the purchaser taps on your item, they will now be taken to an external page.

This is easy to do: for instance, you can do it by utilizing the WordPress-friendly online business module(ecommerce) called WooCommerce. This will permit you to make a store from your site where individuals can see your items. It upholds affiliate content, intending that if somebody taps on a item, they will be taken to the new page utilizing your referral link.

How To Choose a Suitable Drop Shipping Niche

Selecting a Drop shipping niche in which you are interested

Ask yourself, "Am I passionate about anything?" or "If I could buy something right now, what would it be?"

If you are enthusiastic about a certain area, such as gardening, you can utilize that knowledge to select the best items and better serve your clients. Another advantage is that you are more likely to stay motivated when you are not making as many sales.

You can assist your customers by providing them with ideas that you are familiar with or that you discovered while researching that particular subject. This type of material can be used in a newsletter or a blog!

Of course, there must be an audience for the exact area in which you are interested.

For example, you may enjoy creating gluten-free parrot cookies, but you may be the only person who enjoys giving these cookies to their parrot!

So don't forget to use Google Trends or something similar to see if people are interested in your passion.

The niche of hobbies

You will find all of the hobbies of other people this way! Search for 'hobbies' on Google or go to Wikipedia's list of hobbies.

This will give you an idea of the various interests available. After you've chosen several activities that you believe are intriguing, you should see if they're consistent. To put this to the test, go back to Google Trends and enter the name of the hobby.

Investigate Amazon niches

You can find almost everything on Amazon. For example, when writing product descriptions or looking for things to offer.

If you're on Amazon, simply click the "all" button. This will provide you with a long list of potential niches.

To begin, simply select a niche that interests you and press the search button.

Explore AliExpress niches

Another wonderful place to look for potential niches for your store is AliExpress.

Simply hover your cursor over a category to view a plethora of unique ideas.

I have one more tip for you: if you shop on AliExpress, the niches are already divided for you.

1. Home and Garden (The most extensive niche); here you can offer anything from art to furnishings.

2. Kitchen (The middle niche); you can sell anything from bakeware to kitchen tools.

3. Kitchen Gadgets & Tools (The smallest niche); The only thing you can sell currently are kitchen tools and gadgets.

Keep in mind that the larger the niche, the more competition you will face, but this will also mean more clients.

Searching for competition on Facebook

Facebook is an excellent resource for researching potential niches.

Do you know why?

Because if you see Facebook Ads running right now with high engagement and clicks, you know these themes are effective. Because no one would keep a non-profitable advertisement running!

You can also search on Facebook by entering in terms like:

50% / 60% Off (or any other percent off)

Get yours right now / here
Free Shipping
Get It Here
Get It Now
Just Pay Shipping
Click Link
Buy Now
Limited Supply

You can also install Turbo Ad Finder, a free Chrome extension. This will display all of the advertising in your Facebook news feed.

Locating profitable Drop shipping stores

Copying the success of others is another wonderful strategy to locate the greatest niche for your Drop shipping store.

Obviously, you shouldn't imitate everything, but if you discover a large number of successful Drop shipping companies in, say, the pet niche, you might want to try that niche yourself and see if you can match their success!

How to Determine Whether a Drop Shipping Niche Will Be Profitable in 2022

Okay, let me ask you this: did you choose a Drop shipping niche because you are passionate about it or because someone told you it is profitable? So, I'll show you how to determine whether or not your niche will be profitable in 2022.

So, you've compiled a list of potential niches for your Drop shipping store!

Let's see if one of these has a chance to be profitable.

To clarify, when I say profitable, I don't mean that it's a sure bet that you'll make money with that area.

There is a larger possibility that it will become a prosperous Drop shipping niche store than any other niche.

Also, if you do choose a niche, please choose one you are at least a little bit interested in.

1. Look at other Drop shipping stores.

Let's start by seeing if other Drop shipping companies are selling in the niche you're looking at.

What's the best part about looking at other Drop shipping stores?

Inspiration!

There is a good possibility that a niche is profitable if other Drop shipping companies are already selling products in it.

Certainly, if there are numerous Drop shipping stores in your niche.

And if these Drop shipping stores have been around for a while, that's even better.

Why keep a store open if its niche isn't profitable?

Now that you've located some Drop shipping stores in your niche, it's time to see if they're any good.

Why?

Well, if these Drop shipping companies are ordinary Drop shipping stores with nothing remarkable, and they don't appear to be receiving traffic, then it's possible that this niche is not profitable for them.

Another advantage of this is that if you choose a niche where you know who your opponent is, you will know what they are capable of doing better!

How to find out if Drop shipping stores look good

The look of their store. Does it appear that all of them are just standard Drop shipping stores? Then it could be a hint that no money is being made (or that everyone you chose is lazy, so don't take this statement too literally!).

A store like Meowingtons, on the other hand, could be a hint that there is money to be made in that particular market sector.

Their social media accounts. Simply go through all of the social media pages you can locate. Some stores will include a link to them on their website.

You may need to delve a little deeper with others!

Whether you've discovered their social media profiles, check to see if they're receiving a lot of likes and how their postings are doing. Is there a large number of people engaged in your field on that social media platform?

Their Facebook advertisements. Check to see if they have any Facebook Ads running. And, if so, how do they appear? A lot of participation?

Their delivery time. Examine their shipping schedule. Is their shipment time comparable to that of most Drop shippers (between two and four weeks)? Or does it appear that they have a local supplier?

Meowingons, for example, has a very short shipping time to the United States. This could indicate that their business (and niche) are doing well and that they require retail enhancements, such as speedier delivery times.

2. Determine whether or not free traffic is possible.

This is an excellent step.

You'll see if it's possible to gain free traffic in your niche.

Because if there is, you have a good possibility of selling your things through sponsored promotion as well!

a. Google Trends

Let's keep checking Google Trends to see whether people are searching for stuff in your niche.

As you are aware, the dog niche is a consistent niche throughout the year.

This means that this specialization is in high demand throughout the year.

And demand implies the presence of potential clients!

Christmas is another example of this!

Do you hunt for Christmas gifts, decorations, recipes, and so on all year? Or solely during the Christmas season?

I recommend that you explore a few distinct aspects of your niche.

This will give you an excellent idea of whether or not people are looking for your specialty, and if so, for what.

Scrolling down a bit in Google Trends is another excellent technique to determine what your target audience searches for on Google.

There is a lot of information about what kinds of searches and topics are popular!

This is also a good place to go if you're looking for topics to write about in your niche for your store's blog.

If you want to learn more about Google Trends, such as how to use it in your study, read this post for six helpful recommendations!

b. Study social media platforms

The next step is to check social media platforms.

I won't go into specifics about each social media network because the purpose is the same.

The idea is to determine whether or not individuals are active in your niche, as well as the platforms they are most active on.

Facebook Groups

If there are groups within your niche, you can join them to answer questions, add value, and so on.

Try to build a good name for yourself in your niche!

Instagram

The next step is to check Instagram. Check to see how many Instagram pages there are in your niche and how many followers they have.

If so, that's a terrific indication that there are people interested in your niche.

You can also discover if these folks are on Instagram.

You can see this by looking at how many followers the majority of these pages have.

Pinterest

Pinterest is unique in that there are a few niches that will thrive on this social media network.

Pinterest, for example, functions best in the following niches:

Fashion/beauty

Food Auto Home Decoration

Travel Antiques & Collectibles, a significant business dominated by Pinterest

Look at websites like Reddit.

The next step is to see whether there are people on websites like Reddit who can answer questions.

Again, I will not go into depth for each because their purpose is identical.

We're looking to see whether anyone is using these platforms!

And, if yes, do you believe you can acquire free traffic to your Drop shipping store on one (or more) of these platforms?

Reddit

Quora

Forums, like Medium

Youtube

The next step is to look on YouTube to see if there are any popular YouTube channels or videos in the niche you're investigating. Because, as you are aware, video marketing will be critical for ecommerce and Drop shipping shops in 2022!

3. Look into Amazon and AliExpress.

When you were looking for a niche, you most likely visited these websites (or maybe when you were doing product research).

Now I want you to double-check them!

Examine these websites to discover if your niche is selling well.

Are there a lot of dog goods on Amazon, for example?

If you notice a lot of different products within your niche that appear to be drop shippable, and you notice that they are receiving a lot of orders, that's a terrific sign that there is money to be earned in that niche!

The best part is that you can see what sub-niches exist inside your niche:

The following website is worth a look: AliExpress:

Do you observe a variety of products with a high volume of orders?

If that's the case, it's just another indication that people are generating money in that area!

Remember that you don't have to utilize AliExpress for Drop shipping; it's only a starting point to check if people are buying products in your market.

This phase could potentially be combined with your product research!

So, the purpose of this stage is to determine if there are any products in the niche on Amazon or AliExpress (or both), and if so, whether or not they are being sold.

If there are many products accessible and being sold, it could indicate that it is a very profitable niche!

4. Examine paid advertising possibilities

The final and greatest alternative is to investigate paid advertisement choices.

To determine whether a member of your niche is present on these platforms!

Do you comprehend why this is among the best options?

Because there is a high likelihood that you will use paid advertising to promote the products on your Drop shipping website.

Additionally, your paid advertising strategy could benefit from this information.

For instance, do you participate in any interests, hobbies, or similar activities?

Like horticulture or being a parent? You could simply transform this pastime into a specialized Drop-shipping store!

Lastly, if you're new to everything, such as ecommerce and marketing, I advise you to concentrate on a larger area of expertise.

Choosing pets other than simply canines or cats, for instance. This will provide you with a larger "playing field" for experimenting and increase your likelihood of remaining motivated.

You no longer appreciate selling dog products? Not an issue! Just focus on other pets; if you chose a dog business, you would be trapped selling dog products.

Cannot Locate a Drop-shipping Specialty for Your Store?

If you can't think of anything to turn into a Drop shipping store, or if you're unable to find a niche that interests you after conducting research, I suggest beginning with a general Drop shipping store.

You can discover a wealth of beneficial information in this manner. You can always use this in the future to create a specialized Drop shipment store!

Last but not least, if you opt for a general store, you could test, test, and test some more until you discover a winning product, and then build a specialty store/brand around it!

This page contains information on how to test items without spending a lot of money.

Standard Jargon With Which You Should Be Conversant.

Affiliates refer to the website owners who have an affiliate relationship.

• Affiliate sites - These are websites operated by affiliates that feature advertisements and product connections.

• Affiliate marketplace - These are the central registries for various affiliate programs. ShareAsale, Clickbank, and Commission Junction (CJ) are some of these markets.

• Affiliate software: This specialized software is utilized by product merchants or affiliate merchants/networks to create affiliate programs. Among such applications is iDevafilliate.

- Affiliate link: This unique URL generated by affiliate software is provided by an affiliate merchant so that you can track the success of your affiliate program. You should encourage your audience to select this link to obtain the advertised product. Additionally, this URL is used for all other affiliate advertising. You must use this link to ensure that the network platform can record and track your effort; otherwise, your commission will be forfeited.
- Affiliate ID is an identifier that uniquely identifies both you and the product being marketed. Typically, it is incorporated into affiliate links and advertisements.
- Payment method is described by the payment mechanism field. In addition to direct bank transfers, additional payment options include checks, PayPal, and Skrill. It is essential to confirm that the affiliate merchant's payment options

enable you to be paid. If not, save yourself the anguish of pursuing something you cannot have.

• Affiliate marketing with two tiers, also referred to as "double affiliateing." In this case, you are marketing not only products but also a marketplace or platform for affiliates. You can promote products sold through Commission Junction, for example. In addition, you can advertise Commission Junction by encouraging others to become affiliate marketers. It is comparable to the Multi-Level Marketing (MLM) concept.

• Link cloaking - Link cloaking is the process of making an unattractive link more visually appealing by making it easier to scan and comprehend. It also involves safeguarding your connection against intruders.

• Customized coupons - These coupons are branded by affiliate marketers. The product vendor makes them available to the affiliate so that they can be tailored to the target market. The audience may believe that you have exclusive pricing power or a special offer that they cannot find elsewhere, thereby fostering their loyalty and trust. Not all affiliate networks and product sellers offer this functionality. This must be one of the factors considered when selecting the finest product and platform.

• Landing page - A landing page is a page designed specifically to facilitate a single transaction. Therefore, ideally each product should have its own entrance page. However, a product may have multiple landing pages (possibly for special discounts, special offers, a specific audience, etc.). The most common types of landing pages are subscription forms that appear immediately or pages that appear as you navigate down the page. However, a landing page is any page that is specially designed for a particular conversion, regardless of whether it is a pop-up page or not.

The gravitation index measures the percentage of profitable affiliates promoting a particular product. For example, if seven affiliates successfully promote a product, its gravity index will be seven. In contrast, if an additional product is effectively promoted by only two affiliates, its gravitation index will be 2. Consequently, the gravitation index increases with the number of affiliates actively and successfully promoting a product. It should be noted that the gravity index is determined by the number of affiliates who effectively sell a product, and not by the quantity of products sold.

Setting Up A Link Shortening Service

This is an additional important instrument for you if you wish to determine the efficacy of your marketing efforts. In addition to providing you with a shortened URL, a link shortener will also inform you where your traffic is coming from and how many people have clicked on your link.

Bitly is frequently used for this purpose. You can sign up for it for FREE, and it will provide you with the data you need to make the necessary adjustments to your landing page, sign-up forms, advertisements, and email campaigns.

Simply visit Bitly and create a FREE account. Simply enter the extensive URL into the URL shortener, and voila! You will receive a shortened URL along with the option to rename it, making it easier to remember where it leads. The lengthy URL you chose for your landing page should be the first link to be shortened in order to monitor how many people were redirected to it as opposed to how many people joined your mailing list.

Trying to find Facebook Groups

Facebook groups are a great location to connect with other affiliate marketers and share opportunities to enhance your marketing skills.

You probably already have a Facebook profile. Simply enter your topic into the search field, and after the search results appear, select the groups tab to identify the groups. After reviewing the results, ask to join organizations that are related to your field of expertise.

Once you've been granted access to these groups, be sure to read the posted post to determine when you're allowed to post advertisements in order to avoid Facebook jail time.

Once you are familiar with these principles, you may create a list of the groups in which you are permitted to post on specific days. Then, using the resources provided by your affiliate program, select an appropriate image to combine with some original content.

Write approximately three phrases when publishing in these groups to engage the reader. Copy this and your landing page's URL, then publish it with an image in these groups. That's all for the moment. As soon as visitors begin to pour in and your landing page begins to convert, you will begin to see the fruits of your labor.

Why Affiliate Marketing Is The Most Effective Way For Beginners To Generate Income.

Affiliate marketing is one of the most lucrative ways to earn money online. This is a basic, passive, highly scalable, and quick method of making money. You do not need technical expertise, and if you choose the right products and target the right market, you could earn hundreds or thousands of dollars rapidly.

However, let's take a moment to reflect. First, let us define affiliate marketing. How does it operate? What distinguishes it so substantially from other online business income strategies?

Affiliate marketing involves promoting another person's product for a commission. Then, you are compensated per transaction, so all you must do is introduce the product to a market that will find it appealing.

When selling affiliate products such as eBooks, you will frequently discover that you retain 70% or more of the revenue. You can earn the same amount of money by selecting the right product as you would by developing it yourself.

This book will teach you the benefits of affiliate marketing and how to get started swiftly and efficiently so that you can begin earning money. With intelligent product selection, a willing audience, and a little bit of luck.

This book should assist people who are already selling affiliate products by providing them with the additional knowledge and advice they need to advance their business. This includes the strategies employed by prominent brands to market EXPENSIVE products, such as MBA programs and powerful computers costing $5,000 or more.

Many individuals struggle to comprehend the concept of affiliate marketing. How can you make money selling something you did not create?

How is it feasible to earn money online so easily?

It is essentially commerce, to put it in the simplest terms. When you sell something, you act as a vendor and are compensated with a commission. In this regard, you resemble the door-to-door broadband salespeople who visit your home.

The distinction is that you are not knocking on doors. The Internet is your portal, through which you have access to everyone.

On the planet. This gives you an immediate advantage, particularly once you figure out how to attract customers to your company.

In this case, the commission structure will also change significantly, constituting a further distinction. Commonly, salesmen receive a commission of between 5 and 10 percent of what they sell. As stated previously, affiliate marketing differs in that you can earn up to 70–80 percent of sales. As an affiliate marketer, you will frequently earn more than the product's manufacturer!

Affiliate marketing is alluring because it enables you to begin earning money in the same manner as if you were selling your own product, but without having to perform any labor.

In addition, since you will be marketing an existing product, you can select something that is presently performing well. When constructing a product to sell on your own, there is always the possibility that no one will want it. This becomes much less likely when you only market a product that is extremely popular.

The scalability of affiliate marketing is yet another terrific advantage. You can begin earning money from an affiliate product as soon as you create a single web page promoting its benefits.

What therefore prevents you from creating a separate page to promote a different product? Furthermore, another page to market yet another product?

Knowledge of Affiliate Marketing

So, shall we proceed to something more technical? Why would creatives be willing to forego so much of their own revenue, and how does affiliate marketing work?

Let us first consider the type of content you will be selling. For the majority of marketers, affiliate products are digital.

There are additional options that we will investigate later on in this book. However, for the time being, we will focus on that. This consists of materials such as presentations, online courses, and eBooks.

Digital goods are an excellent option for immediate online sales because they have no overhead and no "COGs" (a business term for "Cost of Goods Sold"). Consequently, the author lacks Instead of paying anything for each transaction, they can simply generate profits and divide them among themselves. In addition, they have never had to make a substantial initial investment and they are not responsible for delivery.

Therefore, the creators of this digital product most likely used Microsoft Word or a camera, but it is also possible that they engaged a third party. In any case, they created this eBook or course with the intention of profiting from it.

After that, the creator will likely have begun selling the item via their website or a random online marketplace. To encourage people to purchase from them and generate a passive income stream, they will labor to attract as many website visitors as possible.

However, a person's promotional efforts are limited by their available resources. A creator may then search for affiliates with whom they can collaborate to promote their products.

As a consequence, the product manufacturer is willing to pay affiliates such as us 70% or more to promote their products. In addition, they seek to encourage us to sell their products.

Instead of the products for which other manufacturers offer affiliate programs.

Even though the creator would now receive only 30% of sales, this is still 30% more than if they had resigned.

In addition, the seller will generate immense profits and much more than they could on their own if a swarm of online marketers can attract thousands of people to their books.

Both parties benefit from this situation. As a consequence of the inventor's encouragement of marketers to collaborate with them, a thousand more purchases are made.

Affiliates are permitted to market a product as if it were their own and retain the majority of the sale revenue! They can earn the same amount of money from their own eBook or course without assuming the significant risk of creating one.

This process utilizes "affiliate links" in particular, which rely on cookies to function.

When you locate an affiliate product you wish to market, you will be given an affiliate link; you must use this link on your sales page and in your blog entries.

When a user clicks on your affiliate link, they will be redirected to a new web page. In this case, a cookie identifying them as originating from you will be stored on their computer. Now, whenever they make a purchase from that store, their status as "one of yours" will be recorded, and the commission will be deposited into your account balance for later withdrawal.

You only need to promote the product and provide a link. That's all there is to it!

Utilize Free Report To Boost Affiliate Sales

How to Develop a Free Report – Step-by-Step

Creating complimentary reports to draw attention to affiliate advertisements you wish to highlight is a common practice. The strategy is to create a free report that people want to read and that you can easily distribute to large audiences.

Here are some suggestions to assist you in writing a free report that will attract the interest of Internet users.

Also included are strategies for encouraging readers to click on links within the body of the free proclamation, as well as advertisements that populate the pages of the free report.

One of the initial steps is to deduce the content of your free report. This will be determined in part by the affiliate products you wish to highlight within the text of the report or in the advertisements that accompany the report. Similarly, you want the subject course to be narrow enough so that an informative article can be written, without being overly specific.

As an example, instead of writing a general article about office management, you might choose a topic such as "Seven Effective Ways to Deal with Habitually Late Employees." By concentrating on a single aspect of office management, you benefit in two ways.

First, you have created a topic that will be easily discovered by search engines. Second, you've laid the foundation for an entire series of free announcements that can focus on other aspects of efficient office administration.

People enjoy reading stories, so keep this in mind when crafting your content. This does not imply that you must tell a story for each and every point you make. Just bear in mind that brief examples can illustrate your points while still sounding like a story to the reader. This will encourage your reader to continue reading so he or she can find out what mini-story you present in the next point.

The attentive topic will also allow you to include links and advertisements that are relevant to anyone interested in office efficiency. The placement of links so that they facilitate comprehension throughout the text is extremely valuable.

Stopping to do so will only disrupt the reader's train of thought and likely cause him or her to abandon the page before giving the links and advertisements any consideration. Keep in mind that your revenue from the complimentary announcement will come from people clicking on the links to seller websites or advertisements and, in some instances, purchasing a product.

If the link is properly situated within the text, it will appear almost effortless to click on it and examine the content on the other side.

Publishing your free report can be as simple as offering it on confidential ad sites that allow you to post for free, or as simple as including a link to it in your signature and promoting it on online discussion forums.

You can easily set up a procedure for people to link through to your free report on a web page or receive the free report via email if you use confidential ads sites that generate a substantial amount of traffic.

Keep in mind that psyche-free web pages that permit advertisements on the page and connections in the text are accessible. If you cannot initially afford to set up your website for this type of content, you can generate income and ultimately transfer the free report to your site.

Placing your free announcement online, promoting it on online categorized web sites, and ensuring that it receives massive amounts of susceptibility on forums and ranks well in search engines will make an enormous difference in the success of your free report technique. Why not attempt one today and see what kind of income it generates over the following month?

The Affiliate War: Strategies For Victory

Unlike other conflicts, the ongoing affiliate war CAN be won despite its complexity. In the affiliate battles, lazy affiliate marketers cannot and will not prevail. Affiliate marketing will be won by audacious strategists who are willing to invest a great deal of time and energy.

Affiliate marketing success requires a confident individual. Would you have entered the affiliate marketing battlefield if you knew how intense the competition is? It is immaterial. Right now, you're in the heart of things, and a true warrior simply cannot give up. The only option is to triumph, and to do so magnificently!

To overcome the affiliate marketing conflict, you must win each of the small daily battles and minor skirmishes decisively.

You desire to join this prestigious group of affiliates. You want to be one of those high-earning individuals whose annual salary includes multiple commas in the final figure.

Then, you must be willing to exert considerable effort. You must be willing to go beyond what is required of you. You must be willing to exceed expectations.

In affiliate marketing, reputation is the most crucial factor. There are thousands of affiliate marketers, but only those who have created a name for themselves by becoming highly visible and credible are successful.

Visibility and credibility go hand in hand, and establishing both is crucial to your success and outperforming your competitors.

There are numerous methods for establishing credibility and visibility. Writing and promoting articles and E-books related to your products and services are two of the most important strategies for establishing credibility and visibility. You must demonstrate your status as an authority, or sage, if you will.

You must establish yourself as the individual to whom individuals turn for advice or answers to their questions. Creating articles and e-books (or having them written for you by a ghost writer) is one of the best ways to build your reputation as a knowledgeable individual.

Your original or ghostwritten articles will be posted in repositories where other website owners and E-zine publishers can freely obtain and use them. Each 300–400-word, keyword-rich article will conclude with a resource box containing your name and website address. This facilitates the online discovery of you and your expertise by potential clients.

There should be no more than 10 to 12 pages in an e-book, and each page must contain a link to your website as well as a resource box. Similar to articles, e-books are uploaded to online book repositories where users can obtain and copy them.

It is required that E-Books cannot be altered and that resource box information be included when E-Books are downloaded and replicated for your reputation as an authority in your industry to increase each time they are utilized.

Posting in blogs and forums on topics related to the products and services you sell is another method for boosting your online visibility and credibility. These forums and blogs are simple to locate.

Simply type your pertinent keyword followed by "blogs" or "forums" (+) in the search bar of your preferred search engine. There will be numerous strikes.

Join three or four of the blogs or forums with the most active members and stay with them. Be cautious of this. Effectively posting to blogs and forums will require many hours per week, so limit your selection.

After registering with three or four blogs and forums, you should not immediately begin publishing overt advertisements. Developing credibility and visibility is the objective here.

Behave as if you have recently moved into a new neighborhood and announce yourself. Include your name and a link to your website in the signature element that appears at the end of every post you make.

Take the time to get to know the other forum participants and establish yourself as a valuable team member. You will improve your credibility, exposure, and reputation.

Developing your reputation and credibility takes time. You will be promoting and selling products and services concurrently with their production, and you wish to develop strong relationships with your customers. Ensure that you provide sound advice, superior service, and, if applicable, a guarantee.

Avoid giving your consumers the impression that you are cheap or cutting corners by any means necessary. Customers should be treated with the uttermost respect, as they are your most valuable asset.

Never offer discounts or rebates on products or services. These are not the reputation and clientele you wish to cultivate. Rather than offering discounts or rebates to increase the value of the products and services you're promoting, devise supplementary incentives.

Affiliate battles are won by those who take the trouble and time to establish exemplary reputations as authorities and as ethical and moral merchants.

On the Internet, individuals purchase goods from vendors with whom they are secure conducting business. On the Internet, people purchase products from affiliate marketers with a firm reputation as authorities or gurus and genuine concern for the customers they serve. If you have a reputation for doing honest, diligent work, you will be able to prevail in daily conflicts and, ultimately, the affiliate war.

Your Affiliate Website

Once you've decided which products and/or services you want to promote as an affiliate marketer, it's time to place your ads online.To accomplish this, you will need to create a website, blog, or social media profile, or all three.Since the majority of affiliate programs provide HTML codes for the advertisements that you will display to your users, the majority of affiliate marketers start with a website.

Selecting a Domain Title Creating a website for affiliate marketing is straightforward today.Prior to creating a website, it is essential to choose a domain name that is both memorable and relevant.It is essential to select a domain name that is easy to remember, enunciate, and spell for an affiliate website.The type of products you sell on your website should also be reflected in your domain name.When creating an affiliate website to promote online casinos, you could, for example, choose "toponlinecasinos" or "bestonlinecasinogames" as the domain name.This not only makes it easy for visitors to quickly determine what the website is about, but it is also relevant, simple to pronounce and remember, and SEO-friendly. Given the limited number of.com domain names available, selecting a domain name can be more challenging than you might expect.When selecting a domain name, it is always essential to select.com rather than any other top-level domain.This is because, in addition to the fact that many people still believe there is only a.com extension, it is easier to remember, makes it more difficult to confuse your website with others, and makes it accessible to visitors from all over the world via search engine results.

Configuring Your Website Following the selection of a domain name, the next stage is to create your website.Due to the fact that affiliate ads will be displayed on your website, this phase requires considerable thought, planning, and effort.Your website must not only be visually appealing, but also easy to navigate and quick to launch.Even if you are unfamiliar with HTML or scripting, you can easily create a website using software like WordPress.In this situation, it is recommended to acquire a premium WordPress or other site-creator package so that you can use more themes and make custom modifications to your website.

In order to launch your website, you may also wish to consult with a professional web designer.Paying a professional to design and set up your website is a good option for many affiliate marketers, as they will know which web designs are optimal for affiliate marketing and how to design your website to improve search engine optimization.

Web Hosting If you don't want to use software like WordPress to host your website, you must locate a web host.When selecting a web hosting provider, there are numerous options available, and each must be considered.Here are a few:

Free hosting services that should be avoided at all costs include shared hosting, cloud hosting, virtual private server (VPS) hosting, and dedicated hosting.This is due to the fact that the actual cost of hosting your website is frequently subsidized by advertisements, which could impede your ability to post advertisements on behalf of affiliate programs despite the fact that it is free.In addition to a number of other potential issues that could threaten your business, websites hosted by free hosting providers frequently experience sluggish page load times.

Shared hosting is favored by affiliate marketers due to its generally low price.Using shared hosting, your website will share a server with other websites.Keep in mind, however, that if you choose this option, there is always a chance that your website will be sluggish or inaccessible during peak hours.

In contrast, cloud hosting is a superior option because your website will be hosted on a number of virtual servers, thereby reducing the likelihood of server congestion, and it costs roughly the same as shared hosting.

Virtual private server (VPS) hosting, also known as shared hosting, and dedicated hosting share many similarities.It is less expensive than dedicated hosting, in which your website has its own server, but it provides more storage space than standard hosting.This type of hosting is typically more expensive, so you should only consider it if you believe your business will develop rapidly and require more server space in the future.

There are several essential factors to consider when selecting a hosting service.Included in this is customer service. Choosing a web host with excellent, round-the-clock customer service is essential so that you can rest assured that, if something goes wrong with your website, you will be able to contact the company and have the issue resolved immediately.

Getting Set Up

Web Hosting

If you choose not to host your website using software like WordPress, you will need a web host. When selecting a web hosting company, there are numerous options to choose from, and each must be taken into consideration. These encompass:

Free Hosting
Common Hosting
Hosting in the Clouds
VPS Web Hosting
Exclusive Hosting

No matter how alluring, free hosting must be avoided at all costs. This is because, despite the fact that it will not cost you anything, the actual cost of hosting your website is frequently covered by advertisements, which may conflict with the affiliate program advertisements you place. In addition to a variety of other potential issues that could harm your business, websites hosted by free hosting services tend to render slowly.

Shared hosting is ordinarily quite inexpensive and is favored by affiliate marketers. If you use shared hosting, your website will share a server with other websites. If you choose this option, there is always a possibility that your website will be sluggish or inaccessible during peak hours.

In contrast, cloud hosting, which often costs roughly the same as shared hosting, is the superior option because your website will be hosted on a number of virtual servers, thereby reducing the likelihood of server congestion.

VPS hosting, or virtual private server hosting, is a form of hosting that resembles both shared and dedicated hosting. Although it is less expensive than dedicated hosting, where your website effectively has its own server, it provides more storage space than shared hosting. This type of hosting is typically more expensive and is only appropriate if you anticipate significant growth and the need for additional server capacity in the near future.

Regardless of the type of hosting provider you select, it is essential to keep certain factors in mind. This includes customer service; it is extremely important to choose a hosting provider that offers top-notch, 24/7 customer support so that, if something goes wrong with your website, you can contact them and have the issue resolved.

www.ingramcontent.com/pod-product-compliance
Lightning Source LLC
Chambersburg PA
CBHW050250120526
44590CB00016B/2288